Taylor Swift Quotes Book

Hannah Kurry

"IF YOU'RE LUCKY ENOUGH TO BE DIFFERENT, DON'T EVER CHANGE."

"YOU ARE NOT THE OPINION
OF SOMEONE WHO
DOESN'T KNOW YOU."

"IN A RELATIONSHIP, EACH PERSON SHOULD SUPPORT THE OTHER; THEY SHOULD LIFT EACH OTHER UP."

"ANYTIME SOMEONE TELLS ME THAT I CAN'T DO SOMETHING, I WANT TO DO IT MORE."

"HAPPINESS AND CONFIDENCE ARE THE PRETTIEST THINGS YOU CAN WEAR."

"NO MATTER WHAT HAPPENS IN LIFE, BE GOOD TO PEOPLE. BEING GOOD TO PEOPLE IS A WONDERFUL LEGACY TO LEAVE BEHIND."

"FEARLESS IS NOT THE ABSENCE OF FEAR. IT'S NOT BEING COMPLETELY UNAFRAID. TO ME, FEARLESS IS HAVING FEARS. FEARLESS IS HAVING DOUBTS. LOTS OF THEM."

"THERE ARE TWO WAYS YOU CAN GO WITH PAIN: YOU CAN LET IT DESTROY YOU, OR YOU CAN USE IT AS FUEL TO DRIVE YOU."

"PEOPLE ARE GOING TO JUDGE YOU ANYWAY, SO YOU MIGHT AS WELL DO WHAT YOU WANT."

"IF THEY DON'T LIKE YOU FOR BEING YOURSELF, BE YOURSELF EVEN MORE."

"NEVER BELIEVE ANYONE WHO SAYS YOU DON'T DESERVE WHAT YOU WANT."

"UNIQUE AND DIFFERENT
IS THE NEXT
GENERATION OF BEAUTIFUL."

"IF THEY DON'T LIKE YOU FOR BEING YOURSELF, BE YOURSELF EVEN MORE."

"THERE'S MORE TO LIFE THAN DATING THE BOY ON THE FOOTBALL TEAM."

"BEING FEARLESS ISN'T BEING 100% UNAFRAID. IT'S BEING TERRIFIED BUT YOU JUMP ANYWAY."

"THERE ARE TWO WAYS YOU CAN GO WITH PAIN: YOU CAN LET IT DESTROY YOU, OR YOU CAN USE IT AS FUEL TO DRIVE YOU."

"THE COOLEST THINGS IN LIFE HAPPEN WHEN YOU DON'T LET THE PEOPLE WHO DOUBT YOU BRING YOU DOWN."

"PEOPLE THROW ROCKS AT THINGS THAT SHINE."

"YOU'RE LUCKY ENOUGH TO BE ALIVE IN A WORLD WHERE YOU CAN ANSWER BACK TO PEOPLE WHO DON'T UNDERSTAND YOU."

"ANYTIME SOMEONE TELLS ME THAT I CAN'T DO SOMETHING, I WANT TO DO IT MORE."

"SOMEDAY, I'LL BE
BIG ENOUGH
SO YOU
CAN'T HIT
ME."

"BEING FEARLESS MEANS TAKING CHANCES THAT SCARE YOU, BUT THAT YOU KNOW ARE WORTH IT."

"I THINK THAT YOU CAN LOVE PEOPLE WITHOUT IT BEING THE GREAT LOVE."

"IN A RELATIONSHIP, EACH PERSON SHOULD SUPPORT THE OTHER; THEY SHOULD LIFT EACH OTHER UP."

"IT'S HARD TO FIND YOURSELF WHEN YOU'RE WRAPPED UP IN SOMEONE ELSE."

"SOMETIMES THE PERSON YOU'D TAKE A BULLET FOR IS THE ONE BEHIND THE TRIGGER."

"THE PERFECTION OF LOVE
IS THAT IT'S NOT PERFECT."

“AT SOME POINT, YOU GROW OUT OF BEING ATTRACTED TO THAT FLAME THAT BURNS YOU OVER AND OVER AND OVER AGAIN.”

"THE WAY YOU WALK, WAY YOU TALK, WAY YOU SAY MY NAME – IT'S BEAUTIFUL, WONDERFUL, DON'T YOU EVER CHANGE."

"IN LIFE, YOU LEARN LESSONS.
AND SOMETIMES YOU LEARN THEM
THE HARD WAY. SOMETIMES
YOU LEARN THEM TOO LATE."

"LIFE ISN'T HOW TO SURVIVE THE STORM; IT'S ABOUT HOW TO DANCE IN THE RAIN."

"THE LESSON I'VE LEARNED THE MOST OFTEN IN LIFE IS THAT YOU'RE ALWAYS GOING TO KNOW MORE IN THE FUTURE THAN YOU KNOW NOW."

"THE ONLY WORDS YOU'LL REGRET MORE THAN THE ONES LEFT UNSAID ARE THE ONES YOU USE TO INTENTIONALLY HURT SOMEONE."

"THERE ARE TWO WAYS YOU CAN GO WITH PAIN: YOU CAN LET IT DESTROY YOU, OR YOU CAN USE IT AS FUEL TO DRIVE YOU."

"THE COOLEST THINGS IN LIFE HAPPEN WHEN YOU DON'T LET THE PEOPLE WHO DOUBT YOU BRING YOU DOWN."

"LIFE IS LIKE WALKING; YOU TAKE ONE STEP AT A TIME."

"WORDS CAN BREAK SOMEONE INTO A MILLION PIECES, BUT THEY CAN ALSO PUT THEM BACK TOGETHER."

"YOU CAN'T HAVE A BETTER TOMORROW IF YOU'RE STILL THINKING ABOUT YESTERDAY."

"I THINK I'VE LEARNED THAT
IF YOU KNOW WHAT YOU BELIEVE,
THAT'S ALL THAT MATTERS."

"I WANT TO LEAVE A TRAIL
OF PEOPLE BEHIND ME WHO HAD A
BETTER DAY BECAUSE I WAS THERE."

"THERE IS A TIME FOR SILENCE. THERE IS A TIME FOR WAITING YOUR TURN. BUT IF YOU KNOW HOW YOU FEEL, AND YOU KNOW SO CLEARLY WHAT YOU NEED TO SAY, YOU'LL KNOW IT."

"I THINK IT'S IMPORTANT THAT YOU KNOW THAT I WILL NEVER CHANGE. BUT I'LL NEVER STAY THE SAME EITHER."

"I WANT TO MAKE MUSIC THAT MAKES PEOPLE FEEL GOOD, LIKE THEY'RE NOT ALONE."

"YOU CAN'T CONTROL WHAT PEOPLE SAY ABOUT YOU, BUT YOU CAN CONTROL HOW YOU HANDLE IT."

"I'M INTIMIDATED BY
THE FEAR OF
BEING AVERAGE."

"JUST BE YOURSELF;
THERE IS NO ONE BETTER."

"WE DON'T NEED TO SHARE THE SAME OPINIONS AS OTHERS, BUT WE NEED TO BE RESPECTFUL."

"YOU CAN LET PAIN
DESTROY YOU, OR YOU CAN
USE IT AS FUEL TO DRIVE YOU."

"THERE'S A SPECIAL PLACE IN HELL FOR WOMEN WHO DON'T HELP OTHER WOMEN."

"PEOPLE HAVEN'T ALWAYS BEEN THERE FOR ME, BUT MUSIC ALWAYS HAS."

"PEOPLE ARE PEOPLE,
AND SOMETIMES THEY
CHANGE THEIR MINDS."

"LOVE IS UNPREDICTABLE,
AND IT'S FRUSTRATING,
AND IT'S TRAGIC,
AND IT'S BEAUTIFUL."